OASIS

IN THE

Vale

An Anthology of Poems

Olga Symister

DAYELight
PUBLISHERS

ISBN: 978-1-966723-16-5 (paperback)

Scripture quotations marked "KJV" are taken from the Holy Bible, King James Version (Public Domain).

ACKNOWLEDGMENTS

I give thanks to God, through The Holy Spirit, who has inspired and enabled me to write these poems. I have truly lived and understood the verse in Philippians 4:13, *"I can do all things through Christ which strengtheneth me." (KJV)*. Additionally, He has given me the power to create wealth.

Special thanks to my late husband, Trenton Symister, who encouraged me have my poems published. I guess nothing is done before the time.

To Omar Symister, my son who helped with the technical areas and editing.

To Winnifred Carnegie, my sister, who has always listened as I read some of the poems to her. She encouraged me to write and publish my poems.

Thanks to Norman Scott, who took the headshot; much appreciated.

To all who encouraged me on this journey, thank you.

TABLE OF CONTENTS

Acknowledgments

Rise Up My Soul

Incredible Me

Children Need Your Love And Protection

I Have a Voice—Listen To Me

The Holy Spirit

My Protector

God's Promises

Troublesome Times

I Shall Not Die

Jesus – The Undefeated Champion

I Saw Right Through Him

Church of God, Arise!

Freedom Come Rain

God's Women Shining On

What's Your Identity?

Your Forever Friend

Mothers Are Strong

My Mother

It Is Finished

The Christ of Christmas

Reflections Of Life

About the Author

RISE UP MY SOUL

Arise and bless the Lord, O my soul
Why are you cast down?
Why are you so sad?
When there is hope in God?
Rise up and rejoice—praise Him
With your voice.

Look to the hills; where does your help come from?
Isn't it from the Lord your God?
Doesn't He care for the sparrows when recession hits?
Then rise up my soul; have you forgotten His benefits?

The Lord Your God is your Shield and Defender
He is the lifter of your head; don't you remember?
Jehovah Nissi, your Banner
Jehovah Jireh, your provider
Rise up, rise up, and sing for joy
Bless the Lord, O my soul—Rejoice!

INCREDIBLE ME

Incredible! That's what I am
Special! I'm a part of God's plan
He knew me before I was formed
In my mother's womb—why are you alarmed?
He knows my beginning and also my end
He is my everlasting friend.

Look at me! I was made in His image
To reflect Him in all I envisage
When l lie, He is not pleased
Then I do not reflect Him by any means.

Sometimes I feel bad; I feel very sad
When God is displeased with me
But I go to Him and repent of my sins
And His loving arms again assure me.

Incredible me! that's who I am
I am chosen, I am Christ's, I am called.
Incredible me! that's who I am
I am all a part of God's plan.

CHILDREN NEED YOUR LOVE AND PROTECTION

Children need your love and protection
Just tell me now, what is your intention?
Before we were formed, God knew us
And yet you are wondering, what's the fuss?

We are the future, so treat us right
Don't include us in your fuss and fight
We are impressionable; things are stamped on our minds
When we are treated badly, we, the future, will be in a bind.

We are fearfully and wonderfully made
In the image of God; why should we stand in the shade?
We are born to be leaders; we were born to be great
Our minds God created; only He knows our fate.

God knows our beginning and also our end
He has a plan to give me a hope and a future; didn't you know, my friend?
I'll follow God's plan, as I give Him my hand
Only He knows the way because He has the plan.

We are the future leaders, your prime ministers,

your lawyers
Your pastors, sunday school teachers, your employers
Don't let anyone mistreat us, abuse us, confuse us
We need direction
We, the children, do need your love and protection!

I HAVE A VOICE— LISTEN TO ME

Children must be seen and must not be heard
That's what my mom said happened when she was a girl.
But children nowadays, don't tell them that, my dear.
They will reel off their rights with not the slightest fear.

I have a right to education; I want to go to school!
The Ministry of Education says no corporal punishment—that's the rule.
When I am sick, take me to the doctor
Because if you don't, it could spell disaster.

I must be seen and also heard; I have a voice, so hear my every word.
I need to develop to realize my full potential
I need your protection, as well as your direction.
Let no harm come to my body, mind, or soul
I am your child; please protect me from the cold.

Let no one exploit me; let them not deny me
Let me enjoy life without looking behind me
Let no one abuse me, torment me or use me
God said I'm His heritage, and He will defend me.

Scold me if you must because sometimes that's a
factor
But listen up, and remember that
Children's voices matter.

But just a moment and hear me; I have something
more to say
Although I have rights, the responsibility I must also
take
I must be obedient to my parents
Because they are the ones who will shape,
With the help of the Lord, my character
As our heavenly Father lays it down; so don't forget
this chapter.

We have voices; we must be heard.
but train up the child in the way he should go
Let's do it God's way, and it will be so.

THE HOLY SPIRIT

"I will not leave you comfortless," said Jesus to His friends.
I will send you the Comforter, on whom you can depend.
He'll be your Standby, your Advocate, your Intercessor
Your Counsellor who will teach you all things and can even jog your memory.

Do not let your hearts be troubled, and do not be afraid.
Have confidence in God and trust Him—be brave
Trust in Me as well because I have not lied to you
What you have heard and learned from Me, that you should do.

As the Holy Spirit dwells in you, He will fill you with His power.
You will hear His voice speaking to you; He is your Strong Tower.
He will come alongside you as He gently nudges you.
And teach you the will of God; He's the Spirit of truth.

While I was with you, the Holy Spirit was the power in Me

I did nothing without Him, so neither can you.
Now go and teach My people as you will be empowered.
As the Holy Spirit and fire, I will on you shower.

MY PROTECTOR

I never worry; I just pray
I'm never alone, as the Word of God says
Jehovah Nissi, my Banner and Strong Tower
In Him I hide and will never, ever cower.

The angels of the Lord encamp around me
They form a strong tent, through which the enemy
cannot see.
I am the righteous, and I always run in
To resist the devil whenever he wants to try
anything.

Jehovah Gibbor, strong and mighty in battle
Defends me when the enemy tries to tackle.
The God of heaven's armies is my shield and my
defender
He tells me not to fear, because powerless, He, my
enemy, will render.

So why should I fear when I can stand on His
promises?
They are true, strong, and can never be shaken
The God of gods, the Lord of lords, mighty, powerful
and over all
Jehovah Elohim, the Lord our God, because of Him, I
cannot fall.

GOD'S PROMISES

Healing is the children's bread
That's what the Bible, the good book, says
Jesus gave His life on Calvary
To heal my diseases and set me free.

By His stripes, I have been healed
My confidence in His promises I keep.
I will not waver, I will not fret
My God has never failed me yet.

A lady was bleeding for twelve long years
Suffered a lot, and doctors failed
She heard of Jesus and was determined in her heart
"I must touch Him, whatever the cost!"

Her issue was dried up, as Jesus she touched
Some thought Jesus was making too much fuss
But He turned around and said, "Daughter, you're
healed"
And it happened right there—immediately.

So why should I worry; why should I doubt?
When Jehovah Rapha said, just open your mouth.
I will take sickness from your midst.
When I serve Him, my bread and water He'll bless.

So trust God's promises, they will not fail

"I'll never leave you nor forsake you; do not be afraid."

I will always supply your needs; everything belongs to me

Let not your hearts be troubled, My Shalom will be with thee.

TROUBLESOME TIMES

Abba Father, hear our call
As we, Your children, come to bawl
Our hearts wail, sometimes almost fail
Because of the sorrows down here below
We call on Your mercy to flow.

Brother fighting against brother
Will not try to help each other
Every man for himself
Says there isn't enough food on the shelf
Gracious God, help our calamity
People are deceived over vanity.

Merciful Father, hear our cry
Your children call, they sometimes sigh
We know that You are in control.
We trust You because You look after Your own.
We're the sheep of Your pasture, You'll never leave
We're standing firm, in You, we believe!

Lord, You never failed us yet
Trusting in You, we have no regrets
You are Jehovah Nissi, Our strong and mighty Tower
You stand guard over us every hour
Our God, Jehovah Shalom, is our peace
Our trust in You will never cease.

Lo, I am with you always, in every circumstance,
On every occasion, even to the end of the age.

I SHALL NOT DIE

I shall die but live and declare
The works of the Lord, while I am here.
The number of my days my God set
No man can do anything to shorten—no threat!

He knows my beginning and also my end
God has the blueprint, and will defend
I stand resolute! COVID or not
The blood of Jesus is my solid rock.

I shall not die but live and declare
Why should I fear when Jehovah is here?
His promises are Yea and Amen!
I will stand and trust Elohim
God says, "Fear not, for I am with you.
My Everlasting Arms are right beneath you."

I shall not die but live and declare
Jehovah Gibbor, my warrior, is here.
Ready to defend me, whatever betide
The cables of His heart pass from His heart to mine.
I am the Lord; is anything hard for Me?
I know Who I believe; I am NOT in between
His blood alone is my vaccine!

Hallelujah!

JESUS – THE UNDEFEATED CHAMPION

Undefeated? What is that?
No one's like that, that's a fact
Champions come, and champions go
But none is undefeated
I'm sure you know.

Usain Bolt—undefeated?
Shelly Ann Frazer-Price, what did you say?
Bob Marley—very popular, known around the world
Bunny Grant, Mike McCallumm—sure they were great
But undefeated, no! Let me tell you the One I rate.

Have you heard of a man called Jesus the Christ?
Who walked this earth long ago?
Have you heard of the miracles He performed while He walked?
Making the blind to see, lepers healed while they talked?

Haven't you heard of the Saviour who so loved this world?
That upon a rugged old cross, His body was hurled
He suffered the pain and defeated death
For our sins, He paid with thorns on His head.

Jesus, the Warrior! The King of all kings!
The Everlasting One—of Him do I sing.
He's the undisputed, undefeated champion of love
Forever unchanging, my Master, my Lord.

He defeated death just for my sake.
What do you say to that?
Do you think He is fake?
No, He is the undefeated, undisputed Champion.
Jesus Christ, the only One!

I SAW RIGHT THROUGH HIM

I saw right through him! Yes, I did
When he tried to divide us in his subtle way
When he tried to bring enmity between us
I saw straight through him!
He used the little petty things that don't matter much
To drive a wedge between us.

I saw right through him!
He caused a mountain to be formed out of a molehill
But I saw right through him!
That liar, father of lies, tried to separate us
But I saw straight through him!
He used tactics that I am familiar with, because the Word tells me that I should be aware of his devices.
But I drove him away with "It is written."
I took up the Sword of the Spirit, wielded it in his face
It is written—Love each other as I have loved you.
It is written—if it be possible, live peaceably with all.
It is written—Father, let them be one, as You and I are one.
Yes, the Sword of the Spirit, the Word of God, dealt with him.

He had to run—that liar, that deceiver, that wicked one.
O family, let us not be deceived by our enemy's tactics.
Let us see through him.
He has destroyed lives, families, communities, and countries.
I saw right through him, and I conquered in Jesus Christ's Name!

CHURCH OF GOD, ARISE!

Church of God, let us wake up
Church of God, let us shake up.
Church of God, let us rise.
Aren't we looking in the skies?
The enemy wants to take over
While the people of God are in slumber
Rise up, Church of God, rise up
And shake off dull sloth.

People are dying in their sin
While we are sitting in the sanctuary, cozy and warm
Let's get up, go out and warn
The unsaved are not coming within
They are complaining that the churches look grim.
Let us go out and evangelize
In the streets where they reside.

It is harvest time, people of God
The harvest is plenty, although the reapers are few
We will work overtime to gather souls that are new
Do not let the harvest spoil, do not let them die
Sound the clarion call,
People need Jesus, don't let them fall.

The signs of the times tell us the bridegroom is

coming
Soon His appearing will be; hear the humming?
Men's hearts are failing them for fear as the Word
says
So come, sister, come, brother, we have to work
without fail
God's Word and His people we can't derail
We must reap those souls who are not of this fold
So they will run and come from satan's deadly
stronghold.

Christians awake, Christians arise
Awake from your slumber and reach for the prize
Let us not get caught up in the distraction,
deception, and destruction
We will stand for the truth, so the enemy's lies will
not take root!

FREEDOM COME RAIN

Rain, rain, rain!
Freedom Come Rain.
Two years now, this newspaper a reign
Emancipate yourself, come read a Rain
No meck drought tek you
When you can soak in this rain.

Wey you did deh why you neva know bout dis rain?
No wonder you always a feel all kinds of pain
You sit and cry, Lord, what happened to me?
Why is my soul in so much drought?
A beg you come by me.

You ask, what to expect in the Freedom Come Rain?
So many things you will have to gain
Pastor's prayers, you nuh waan miss that
Recipes galore for the foodie them; What?

Yes, man, come. Come wet up yourself.
The doctor in the place
You nuh have fe run nuh race.
The dentist is here to give you good advice
About your teeth and help you to decide.

I can't tell you everything in the Rain
All I know is that the children will also gain
Because schoolwork in there and fun page too

Just take a look; you have nothing to lose.

So, run come quick; come buy you Rain newspaper
You can get it anywhere around the nation
Supermarkets,   pharmacies,   gas   stations—
everywhere
No meck drought ketch you
Because the Rain is here!

GOD'S WOMEN
SHINING ON

We are the light of the world; come let us shine!
People can't see because they are blind
The enemy, the devil, has placed a mask
On the minds of men to lure them in the dark.

He's like a roaring lion, seeking to devour
Men and women, so let's not cower.
We need to bloom where we are planted
So, as we go, let's not be daunted by the enemy who comes to steal
We will go out there and try to heal.

Let us gird our armour on and stand firm; stand resolute!
The enemy will realise that we are not just cute
We are not retreating when he comes to steal
We are wielding the Sword of the Spirit, for we are conquerors—don't yield
The Word says to resist him and he must flee
He has already been defeated, that's our guarantee.

Let's glow ladies, glow in the darkness that surrounds us
Lovingly, let us draw others to Jesus
Obedient to the call of God

OLGA SYMISTER

Women, God's women, shining on!

WHAT'S YOUR IDENTITY?

Men looking like women
Women looking like men
Lost your identity, my friend?
There is so much confusion; when will it end?

When God made Adam and Eve
He said, "Very good, very good!"
Be fruitful and multiply, bear children, and fill the earth
There's enough food to go around
East, west, north, and south.

Two males equals no children
Two females – Oh no! Can't procreate
The animals went in the ark, male and female
So they could continue to multiply without fail.

The human race could one day become extinct
If male and female are not linked.
We would have to use robots to do all the work
What a something that would be on the earth!

Why do we want to rewrite creation?
Wiping out people in the nations?
Humans are trying to replace God
Using science and technology, how sad!

God is in control – no matter how hard they try.
Science has its place, but won't reach the skies.
Man has been given the wisdom to be creative
But flying in God's face is very abrasive.

God is to be feared; He is Sovereign
Let's stay in our sphere and serve Him with reverence
Let us know our gender, and multiply
Serving God who has created life.

YOUR FOREVER FRIEND

Young man, sitting on the corner
Rubbing out your hand middle, seeking for answers
Have you found it in that substance?
Don't you realize there's only One in whom you can
put your confidence?

Young lady, the answer's not in a man
Looking for someone to give you validation
Searching in places that will only bring you
frustration
There's hope—if you turn around—you wouldn't
ruin your reputation.

Young person, you were fearfully and wonderfully
made
By God, your Father, who loves you without fail
You were bought at a price that you never could pay
So run in His arms and acknowledge Him in all your
ways.

You are loved so unconditionally
By your heavenly Father, who has you in His palms.
He says, "Seek Me first, and I will give you all you
require
A home in My kingdom; what more can you desire?

Seek the Lord today, whether you're in Kingston or

Mobay
His love is everlasting
His kindness is unsurpassing
You'll wonder, "Why didn't I know Him long ago?"
Your Saviour, your Love, He will make you glow!

MOTHERS ARE STRONG

Mothers are strong, though some think they're weak
Mother, you're strong; you just can't be beat
Mother, I love you. God gave you to me
Mother, O Mother, my friend.

You carried me for nine months, then when I was born
You brought me up just as the Lord would want
You hugged me, kissed me, and corrected me when I was rude
For God has commanded that you should.

Mother, there are nights when you cry to the Lord
To guide your child and keep me safe from all harm
It gives me comfort just to know that you pray
That angels will guide me every day.

Mothers are built with a special machine
That manufactures tears to cry over me
You cry when I'm sad; you cry when I'm sick
You cry when the doctor says, "I've got to be stitched."

Mother, there are times when I make you so mad
Please forgive me; I love you and forever will be glad
That I have a mother who is so kind and loving
Lord, help me, I pray, and make me Your own.

MY MOTHER

A mother's love knows no bounds
All her qualities are sound
She wakes up in the night and prays
For all her children, that God would keep them in His ways.

A disciplinarian was she
Her motto from the Bible is and will always be
"Spare not the rod and spoil the child."
Don't let them grow up and run wild.

A cross look from the cradle was her mantra
The rod of correction was not propaganda
She loved her children all
But sought to train them in God's way so they would not fall.

Mother did not eat the bread of idleness
She worked hard to make sure we were always blessed.
Church was a MUST, for her children—no fuss.
Early morning devotion was always her motion.

She had a poem or story for every situation.
Wisdom was handed down from generation to generation
She was not a top scholar, but that did not matter

But her wisdom and council to others was an anchor.

Kindness was my mother's very nature
She would give away her last cracker to her neighbor
Everyone called on her for help
Although sometimes she had a small amount for her family and herself.

Mother, you did not spare the rod and spoil your children
But we grew up with many good lessons.
Waste not, want not. One one coco full basket
Were among the many lessons that she taught us
Mother, your life and examples have drawn us to God.

IT IS FINISHED

Betrayed by a friend, denied by a brother
Cried in the garden: If it be possible, let this cup pass
He came to die because it was God's will
For man's redemption to be fulfilled.

Boxed and beaten, bruised and torn
Spat upon and cursed, despised and rejected
A Man of sorrow, He was acquainted with grief
He was the middle Man crucified between two thieves.

In Pilate's judgment hall, He stood quite tall
Not caring to answer His accuser at all
"Do you not know I have the power," said Pilate
"To kill You or release You from Your accusers who crave You?"

You would have no power unless it be given you
My kingdom is not here, or My soldiers would destroy you
So, You are a King! Indeed we will crown you!
So, a thorny crown He wore just to pay the price for you.

The crowd cried, "Crucify! Away with Him; let Him die!
We have not a king; take Him to Golgotha's hill!

Let Him carry His own cross; let us see how he fares."
He was scourged with many stripes
Ridiculed by those standing there.

He was nailed upon the cross, clothes parted for by lots
His thorny crown pressed down, blood flowing from His brow
Why did He die for me? Did I deserve such love?
But when He said, "It's finished,"
My redemption was sealed from above.

I have accepted Him as my personal Lord and Saviour
How could I such a Friend reject, when He gave His life to save me?
May I invite you right now, too, to give your life to Jesus
There will be no regrets—only a new life and happiness.

THE CHRIST OF CHRISTMAS

Where is Christ, if not in Christmas?
Where is Christ? He is a must!
Christmas pageants, Christmas trees, Christmas candles, Christmas teas
Christmas presents, Christmas clothes, Christmas parties all night long.

We give gifts to everyone during this special season,
Shops and houses are decorated, but what is the reason?
There are all the bells and trimmings
And people prepare the gifts they are giving
But never really remembering,
The One they should be honouring.

Why did the angels come? Giving glad tidings to some?
Who was that tiny Babe in that lowly cradle of hay?
It was because of the Christ Child that came to earth to die.
Let's put Christ back in Christmas
The One who gave His life for us!

REFLECTIONS OF LIFE

Young and full of vigour and energy
No thought of getting elderly.
There were up times and down days
But there was no thought that separation would
come one day.

Thirty-five years together seems a long time
All started when we were in our prime.
Children come running around the house
Having a good time with your spouse.

There were arguments and heated discussions
But agree to disagree was always the mission
Prayer had to be an integral part of the process
Because without God, there would be no success.

As the years went by, and empty nest took over
You wonder where the years went, and you become
sober
You start to reminisce about the days when you had
to dress a cut
And took your child out of a rut.

Now you have reached the top of the mountain
You are on the other side and counting
Life has been good; God has taken you here
Praise His name and be of good cheer.

"I will never leave you," that's what He says.
His promises are yes and amen; you can trust them
always.
The number of your days He will fulfil
Just lean on Abba and do His will.

ABOUT THE AUTHOR

Olga Symister, servant of the Most-High God, El-Elyon, is a mother of one adult son, Omar. She is a retired primary school teacher. She is involved in several areas of her church—a Sunday School teacher, sings in the choir, and Women's Fellowship President.

Olga started out writing a few songs for the Sunday School choir, of which she was co-director, and one for the fiftieth anniversary of her church. Writing poems is a latent talent that the Lord has given her. She started out by writing poems for children to do during Child's Month celebrations, and from there, the Holy Spirit just gave her the inspiration to write. She would be sitting or lying down, and some words just come to her. She would take up her pen and start writing. She also writes out of situations that may arise.

In the classroom, poems and songs were part of the strategy she employed to get children to enjoy the lessons, which helped the learning process.

These poems have been written over many months, and she was always encouraged by her late husband to have them published. Nothing happens before the time. She also enjoys reading and watching Christian movies. She hopes that whoever reads these poems will find them enjoyable, reflective and contemplative.

"I can do ALL things through Christ who strengthens me." (Philippians 4:13 - KJV)